Vikram Seth

All You Who Sleep Tonight

Vikram Seth was trained as an economist. He has lived for several years each in England, California, China, and India; the poems in the present volume reflect his understanding of these four cultures. He is the author of an earlier book of poems, *The Humble Administrator's Garden*, as well as the novel in verse, *The Golden Gate*. *From Heaven Lake* is an account of his travels through Sinkiang and Tibet. He has just completed a book of translations from three Chinese poets of the Tang Dynasty, and is working on a novel (not in verse) set in post-Independence India.

INTERNATIONAL

BOOKS BY VIKRAM SETH

Poems

All You Who Sleep Tonight   1990
The Golden Gate (*A Novel in Verse*)   1986
The Humble Administrator's Garden   1985
Mappings   1980

Nonfiction

From Heaven Lake: Travels Through Sinkiang and Tibet   1983

All You Who Sleep Tonight

All You Who Sleep Tonight

Poems by Vikram Seth

Vintage International
Vintage Books
A Division of Random House, Inc.
New York

First Vintage International Edition, April 1991

Copyright © 1987, 1990 by Vikram Seth

All rights reserved under International and Pan-American Copyright Conventions. Published in the United States by Vintage Books, a division of Random House, Inc., New York, and simultaneously in Canada by Random House of Canada Limited, Toronto. Originally published by Alfred A. Knopf, Inc., New York, in 1990.

Acknowledgments

Three poems from the section *In Other Voices* were directly inspired by passages from the following books: *Ghalib: Life and Letters* by Ralph Russell and Khurshidul Islam (Harvard University Press); *Commandant of Auschwitz* by Rudolf Hoess (Weidenfeld); *Hiroshima Diary* by Michihiko Hachiya (The University of North Carolina Press).

Poems from this work were originally published in the following publications:

London Magazine: "Suzhou Park"
Numbers: "Lithuania: Question and Answer," "How Rarely These Few Years,"
     "A Style of Loving"
PN Review: "Heart," "The Scent of Sage and Bay"
Poetry Review: "The Stray Cat"
Scripsi: "Walk"
Spectator: "Work and Freedom"
Threepenny Review: "On the 50th Anniversary of the Golden Gate Bridge"
Times Literary Supplement: "Protocols"

Library of Congress Cataloging-in-Publication Data
Seth, Vikram, 1952–
All you who sleep tonight : poems / by Vikram Seth.—1st
Vintage International ed.
p. cm.—(Vintage international)
ISBN 0-679-73025-7
I. Title.
[PR9499.3.S38A79   1991]
821—dc20   90-50627
              CIP

Author photograph © Aradhana Seth

Manufactured in the United States of America
10 9 8 7 6 5 4 3 2 1

For Shantum *and* Aradhana

Contents

CONTENTS

I *Romantic Residues*

After a long and wretched flight
That stretched from daylight into night,
Where babies wept and tempers shattered
And the plane lurched and whiskey splattered
Over my plastic food, I came
To claim my bags from Baggage Claim.

Around, the carousel went around.
The anxious travelers sought and found
Their bags, intact or gently battered,
But to my foolish eyes what mattered
Was a brave suitcase, red and small,
That circled round, not mine at all.

I knew that bag. It must be hers.
We hadn't met in seven years!
And as the steel plates squealed and clattered
My happy memories chimed and chattered.
An old man pulled it off the Claim.
My bags appeared: I did the same.

What can I say to you? How can I now retract
    All that that fool, my voice, has spoken—
Now that the facts are plain, the placid surface cracked,
    The protocols of friendship broken?

I cannot walk by day as now I walk at dawn
    Past the still house where you lie sleeping.
May the sun burn away these footprints on the lawn
    And hold you in its warmth and keeping.

Light now restricts itself
To the top half of trees;
The angled sun
Slants honey-colored rays
That lessen to the ground
As we bike through
The corridor of Palm Drive.
We two

Have reached a safety the years
Can claim to have created;
Unconsummated, therefore
Unjaded, unsated.
Picnic, movie, ice cream;
Talk; to clear my head
Hot-buttered rum—coffee for you;
And so not to bed.

And so we have set the question
Aside, gently.
Were we to become lovers
Where would our best friends be?
You do not wish, nor I
To risk again
This savored light for noon's
High joy or pain.

Across these miles I wish you well.
May nothing haunt your heart but sleep.
May you not sense what I don't tell.
May you not dream, or doubt, or weep.

May what my pen this peaceless day
Writes on this page not reach your view
Till its deferred print lets you say
It speaks to someone else than you.

It's evening. I lack courage.
The sun has set behind the fogbound hill.
The breeze has died, even the jays are silent.
The lake is still.

I sit down. I am tired.
To speak my mind's beyond my power to do.
I have no warranty against the vision
I have of you.

You're close, and cannot help me.
The concrete slab is cold. The arcing stars
Pass too high overhead for easy grasping
Even if ours.

But frogs' songs, quiet ripples,
These we may claim, and for this while concede
We are, at least in hope, unequal equals,
If not in deed.

I smiled at you because I thought that you
Were someone else; you smiled back; and there grew
Between two strangers in a library
Something that seemed like love; but you loved me
(If that's the word) because you thought that I
Was other than I was. And by and by
We found we'd been mistaken all the while
From that first glance, that first mistaken smile.

Sit, drink your coffee here; your work can wait awhile.
You're twenty-six, and still have some of life ahead.
No need for wit; just talk vacuities, and I'll
Reciprocate in kind, or laugh at you instead.

The world is too opaque, distressing, and profound.
This twenty minutes' rendezvous will make my day:
To sit here in the sun, with grackles all around,
Staring with beady eyes, and you two feet away.

After a few short bars
You stop and look at me.
The last of our few hours
Is over. I am free.

Free now to leave this room,
Its broken chords, its light,
Its scent of lilac bloom,
And be elsewhere tonight.

You wrestle for reserve
And its keen dignity.
Now is the time to serve
Eviction upon me.

"I will not see you out.
I hope you understand."
Only your mouth speaks doubt.
I take your chordless hand.

I see my younger grief
Accusing with your eyes.
I cannot give relief
Nor can you give me lies.

But do not say I've wrecked
Your peace and caused you pain.
I've done that, I suspect,
But won't do so again.

You see me to the street.
The cars slosh past. It's true
That I may have light feet.
I'm not in love with you.

And yet with half my heart
I wish I were—that we,
Knowing that we must part,
Could share this equally.

Great city, harsh and tall,
In the cold throes of spring—
Numb and distract us all
That love may lose its sting.

A cab. You take my hand,
Then stand and frown awhile.
At my express demand
You undertake to smile.

I walked last night with my old friend
Past the old house where we first met,
Past each known bush and each known bend.
The moon shone, and the path was wet.

No one passed by us as we strolled
At our sad ease. Though hand in hand
We did not speak. Our hands grew cold,
Yet we walked on as we had planned.

We did not deal in words or tears.
At the dead light we did not rage.
What change had crept through our forked years
We did not have the will to gauge.

The lights went out. Who lived here now,
Paid rent, and saw spring come and go
Lived past the range of why and how
For those who had no wish to know.

II *In Other Voices*

TO WEI BA, WHO HAS LIVED AWAY FROM THE COURT

translated from the Chinese of Du Fu

Like stars that rise when the other has set,
For years we two friends have not met.
How rare it is then that tonight
We once more share the same lamplight.
Our youth has quickly slipped away
And both of us are turning gray.
Old friends have died, and with a start
We hear the sad news, sick at heart.
How could I, twenty years before,
Know that I'd be here at your door?
When last I left, so long ago,
You were unmarried. In a row
Suddenly now your children stand,
Welcome their father's friend, demand
To know his home, his town, his kin—
Till they're chased out to fetch wine in.
Spring chives are cut in the night rain
And steamed rice mixed with yellow grain.
To mark the occasion, we should drink
Ten cups of wine straight off, you think—
But even ten can't make me high,
So moved by your old love am I.
The mountains will divide our lives,
Each to his world, when day arrives.

To Ephraim Oshry, rabbi, this is the case:
A woman of a good family in Kovno
Came to me weeping, comfortless. The Germans
Had raped her and had tattooed on her arm
The legend, "Whore for Hitler's troops." She found
Her husband recently, and they intended
To build again a proper Jewish home
(Their children had been killed). But when he saw
The words he was appalled, and felt constrained
To ask, "Is she permitted me or not?
Was there consent in this?" She came to me,
Eyes asking mercy. Tell me what to do.

This took place in the city, not the field.
Nor did she cry out, therefore we may assume
That she consented. But Maimonides
Has said a sword above the head spells force.
Would it avail her to cry out? A sword
Was over all our heads. She could not wish
To lie with the abominable wolves.

This leads to the conclusion in this case
That she was forced. For in addition to
What we have used above, some others say
Even in the city with no witnesses
Such words are to be trusted.

Far be it
From anyone to cast aspersion on
These honorable women. He who hears
The pleadings of the poor will heal their sorrow.
I know that some men have divorced such wives.
Alas for us this happens in our times.

Preserve those words. They bear no tint of shame.
They will remind you that we yet shall see
The fall of the transgressors from whose face
Is blotted any human semblance—wolves,
Beasts of the forest and voracious wolves
Who hasten to spill innocent blood and kill
The pious and the upright. Read those words
But think of Moses' words, the man of God:
"Sing aloud, O you nations, of His people;
For he avenges the blood of his servants, and
Renders revenge upon His adversaries."

Even small events that others might not notice,
I found hard to forget. In Auschwitz truly
I had no reason to complain of boredom.
If an incident affected me too deeply
I could not go straight home to my wife and children.
I would ride my horse till the terrible picture faded.
Often at night I would wander through the stables
And seek relief among my beloved horses.
At home my thoughts, often and with no warning,
Turned to such things. When I saw my children playing
Or observed my wife's delight over our youngest,
I would walk out and stand beside the transports,
The firepits, crematoriums, or gas chambers.
My wife ascribed my gloom to some annoyance
Connected with my work—but I was thinking,
"How long will our happiness last?" I was not happy
Once the mass exterminations had started.

My work, such unease aside, was never-ending,
My colleagues untrustworthy, those above me
Reluctant to understand or even to listen—
Yet everyone thought the commandant's life was heaven.
My wife and children, true, were well looked after.
Her garden was a paradise of flowers.
The prisoners, trying no doubt to attract attention,
Never once failed in little acts of kindness.
Not one of them, in our house, was badly treated:
My wife would have loved to give the prisoners presents—
And as for the children, they begged for cigarettes for them,

Especially for those who worked in the garden and brought
   them
Tortoises, martens, lizards, cats. Each Sunday
We'd walk to the stables, never omitting the kennels
Where the dogs were kept. My children loved all creatures
But most of all our foal and our two horses.
In summer they splashed in the wading pool, but their greatest
Joy was to bathe together with Daddy—who had
Limited hours, alas, for these childish pleasures.
My wife said, "Think of us, not only the service."
How could she know what lay so heavily on me?
(It made life hard, this excessive sense of duty.)

When Auschwitz was divided, Pohl in a kindly
And quite exceptional gesture gave me the option
—Perhaps as recompense for this last assignment—
To head DK or to run Sachsenhausen.
I had one day to decide. At first the thought of
Uprooting myself from Auschwitz made me unhappy,
So involved had I grown in its tasks and troubles.
But in the end I was glad to gain my freedom.

Dear Yusuf Mirza, none but God can know my plight.
Men have gone mad from cares far less than those I fight.
But grief and cares for what? you ask—what do I claim?—
For death, for parting, for my livelihood, my name.

Whose deaths? I leave aside the stricken Mughul court;
In Delhi proper—not the Inauspicious Fort—
Your uncle; Ashur Beg; and Mir Nāsir-ud-din;
My sister's grandson too, a mere child of nineteen;

Mustafa Khan; his sons; the blood flows from my pen.
The names go on; O God! What can replace such men?
Those of my friends who live, like Miran and Majruh,
Condemned to roam the world, may God preserve them too.

My brother died insane; his children and his wife,
Stranded in Jaipur, eke their pittance of a life.
The children of high lords go begging in the street.
My household, God knows how, finds just enough to eat.

Nor is my time my own. I have grown old. How can
I bear this load? I am no giant but a man.
I leave my sickbed, try to sit an hour or two
To write, to plan, to think—but there's too much to do.

As for sustaining wine, my cash won't spill that far—
Still less to buy a gift if called to the durbar.
They used to call me once. Will they do so again?—
I who have neither helped nor harmed the Englishmen.

I'm sending you an ode about my life, which night
And day for two long months I've sweated blood to write.
Say if you think my skill has cheated fortune's knife
Even if my heart lacks fire—why fire? even life.

In my old eulogy, for Amjad Ali's name
I've slotted "Wājid" in; but God has done the same.
Such verse in praise of kings, just notch it down a peg:
I wrote it not to show my prowess but to beg.

More news. That gentle boy, Shivji Ram's son and pride,
Fell ill, lay two days thus, and on the third day died.
His father is distraught with grief, and for my part
I have lost two more friends, one dead, one sick at heart.

Another twenty months, and I too will be dust:
My body to Rampur, my soul to light, I trust.
What grief, joy, praise or shame afflict me in this spell
I will find strength to face. Goodbye. May all be well.

The morning stretched calm, beautiful, and warm.
Sprawling half-clad, I gazed out at the form
Of shimmering leaves and shadows. Suddenly
A strong flash, then another, startled me.
I saw the old stone lantern brightly lit.
Magnesium flares? While I debated it,
The roof, the walls and, as it seemed, the world
Collapsed in timber and debris, dust swirled
Around me—in the garden now—and, weird,
My drawers and undershirt had disappeared.
A splinter jutted from my mangled thigh.
My right side bled, my cheek was torn, and I
Dislodged, detachedly, a piece of glass,
All the time wondering what had come to pass.
Where was my wife? Alarmed, I gave a shout,
"Where are you, Yecko-san?" My blood gushed out.
The artery in my neck? Scared for my life,
I called out, panic-stricken, to my wife.
Pale, bloodstained, frightened, Yecko-san emerged,
Holding her elbow. "We'll be fine," I urged—
"Let's get out quickly." Stumbling to the street
We fell, tripped up by something at our feet.
I gasped out, when I saw it was a head:
"Excuse me, please excuse me—" He was dead:
A gate had crushed him. There we stood, afraid.
A house standing before us tilted, swayed,
Toppled, and crashed. Fire sprang up in the dust,
Spread by the wind. It dawned on us we must

Get to the hospital: we needed aid—
And I should help my staff too. (Though this made
Sense to me then, I wonder how I could
Have hoped, hurt as I was, to do much good.)
My legs gave way. I sat down on the ground.
Thirst seized me, but no water could be found.
My breath was short, but bit by bit my strength
Seemed to revive, and I got up at length.
I was still naked, but I felt no shame.
This thought disturbed me somewhat, till I came
Upon a soldier, standing silently,
Who gave the towel round his neck to me.
My legs, stiff with dried blood, rebelled. I said
To Yecko-san she must go on ahead.
She did not wish to, but in our distress
What choice had we? A dreadful loneliness
Came over me when she had gone. My mind
Ran at high speed, my body crept behind.
I saw the shadowy forms of people, some
Were ghosts, some scarecrows, all were wordless, dumb—
Arms stretched straight out, shoulder to dangling hand;
It took some time for me to understand
The friction on their burns caused so much pain
They feared to chafe flesh against flesh again.
Those who could, shuffled in a blank parade
Towards the hospital. I saw, dismayed,
A woman with a child stand in my path—
Both naked. Had they come back from the bath?
I turned my gaze, but I was at a loss
That she should stand thus, till I came across
A naked man—and now the thought arose

That some strange thing had stripped us of our clothes.
The face of an old woman on the ground
Was marred with suffering, but she made no sound.
Silence was common to us all. I heard
No cries of anguish, or a single word.

I shall die soon, I know.
This thing is in my blood.
It will not let me go.
It saps my cells for food.

It soaks my nights in sweat
And breaks my days in pain.
No hand or drug can treat
These limbs for love or gain.

Love was the strange first cause
That bred grief in its seed,
And gain knew its own laws—
To fix its place and breed.

He whom I love, thank God,
Won't speak of hope or cure.
It would not do me good.
He sees that I am sure.

He knows what I have read
And will not bring me lies.
He sees that I am dead.
I read it in his eyes.

How am I to go on—
How will I bear this taste,
My throat cased in white spawn—
These hands that shake and waste?

Stay by my steel ward bed
And hold me where I lie.
Love me when I am dead
And do not let me die.

III *In Other Places*

Sudden and swift I hear
A distant avalanche.
The last stars disappear.
The blue snows flush and blanch.

As shadows, then as mass,
The mountains of Garhwal
Serrate and curve by pass
And peak towards Nepal.

The rising mist now fills
The forest rifts below:
Peninsulas of hills
And lakes of fluid snow.

Oak, rhododendron, pine
And cedar freed from night
Recede in a design
As visionless as white.

Magnolia trees float out their flowers,
Vast, soft, upon a rubbish heap.
The grandfather sits still for hours:
His lap-held grandson is asleep.
Above him plane trees fan the sky.
Nearby, a man in muted dance
Does tai-qi-quan. A butterfly
Flies whitely past his easy trance.
A magpie flaps back to its pine.
A sparrow dust-rolls, fluffs, and cheeps.
The humans rest in a design:
One writes, one thinks, one moves, one sleeps.
    The leaves trace out the stenciled stone,
    And each is in his dream alone.

A glass of tea; the moon;
The frogs croak in the weeds.
A bat wriggles down across
Gold disk to silver reeds.
The distant light of lamps.
The whirr of winnowing grain.
The peace of loneliness.
The scent of imminent rain.

Like life, there is a plan but little sense.
Each step, each cryptic path, each stone and plane,
Each thwarting twist implies intelligence
Far more than playful and far less than sane.
Yet children love it, gulp with shocking glee
When parents, desperate that they may have drowned,
Hunt through the pool-pierced maze of masonry
And are too pleased for anger when they're found.

She looked at him, he at the guide.
The facts rolled on; they walked outside
To where confinement seemed less dense,
Breath quieter, rinsed of the pretense
Of the group-jollity that swore
And clucked and posed and clicked before
The turtle stele. The last light
Eased them as travelers into night.

They did not speak the language though
They'd lived here forty years ago
In hopeless times and cleaner air
And had been happy. A despair
Of change had led them back again,
Though group-contained, to an old scene.
Yet now the unaltered steps had made
Him breathless, her therefore, afraid.

There on the Drum Tower, sipping tea,
They watched the sun set lingeringly
Across the black bricks, leaves and dust
That were the city. They discussed
Their next day's pre-planned enterprise
And turned their unexpectant eyes
To where, smoke-red and unentire,
There glowed out an uncertain fire.

Here by the sea this quiet night
I see the moon through misted light.
The water laps the rocks below.
I hear it lap and swash and go.
The pine trees, dense and earthward-bent,
Suffuse the air with resin-scent.
A landward breeze combs through my hair
And cools the earth with salted air.

Here all attempt in life appears
Irrelevant. The erosive years
That built the moon and rock and tree
Speak of a sweet futility
And say that we who are from birth
Caressed by unimpulsive earth
Should yield our fever to the trees,
The seaward light and resined breeze.

Here by the sea this quiet night
Where my still spirit could take flight
And nullify the heart's distress
Into the peace of wordlessness,
I see the light, I breathe the scent,
I touch the insight, but a bent
Of heart exacts its old designs
And draws my hands to write these lines.

He fingers his dark rosary
And sounds the gong, again, again,
Blinks at the flash photography
Of the grave Japanese businessmen.
They leave. He turns and, with a smile,
Asks me, *Are Indian people poor?*
Are they all Buddhist? In a while
He talks about the Gang of Four.
*Ten years—we were sent down—*He stares
In contemplation at a face,
Gold, calm, unsorrowing, that bears
Pain, age, death, vandals, and disgrace—
Then sees my puzzled eyes, and brings
Himself to earth, and milder things.

The gray Pacific, curved and old,
    Indented, bare,
Flings out, day after day, its cold
    Breakers to where

Marin and San Francisco shore
    The rapid strait
Christened a century before,
    The Golden Gate.

Both counties know this still might be
    A wistful view
If Strauss had not resolved to see
    The matter through.

Though courts twice threatened it, though storms
    Once washed away
The trestles of his bridge, two forms
    Inched day by day

Closer so that the ocean's rift
    Might disappear.
Two stubborn decades were his gift;
    He died next year.

How fortunate such greatness stirred
    In his small frame
That even obstacles deferred
    To set his fame.

PS 301 - 326

PS 580 - 619

PT 7000s -
   9000s

Audrey Lorde

Paul Celan

George

Patron

_____

Pull Date _____

HOLD

FOR

1 WEEK

How sad that he should be so small
	In his great mind
To disacknowledge after all
	Him who designed

This shape of use and loveliness
	And to subject
Ellis, his partner in success,
	To long neglect.

Two towers hold the cable; ton
	On ton of it
Hangs chainlike from their peaks, yet one
	Alone is lit.

But let us leave blurred facts behind
	In the plain hope
That each will be at last assigned
	His equal scope

—A claim that justice can in no
	Clear light refuse—
And glimpse the fifty years that flow
	Down from those views.

How much of life has passed above,
	Below, upon.
How much of hatred and of love
	Has come and gone!

What portion of the soldiers who
    Sailed out to war
Sailed back beneath the bridge they knew
    Four years before?

How many lovers who have found
    A world of mist
To cloak them from the world around
    Have stood and kissed

Where others, who have walked alone
    On a bright day,
In unsupported grief have thrown
    Their lives away.

How many more have been impelled
    From death they craved,
By force or by persuasion held,
    And somehow saved.

"I would have been happy and dead,
    I'm sure, by now,
If it weren't for those heroes," said
    One saved somehow.

And surely, if one had to die,
    What happier place
To quit that over-salted pie,
    The human race?

Indeed this morning's pilgrimage
 Just after light
Saw us frail lemmings on the bridge
 Jammed in so tight,

Breathing against a neighbor's face,
 Gasping for air,
We almost quit the human race
 Right then and there.

But panic could not scuttle love,
 A love half-blind,
An amiable affection of
 A civic kind

For what we've known for years, for all
 Who feel the same,
As when in darkness we recall
 A common name.

It is as if the bridge's core,
 Its grace, its strength
Could not have not been on this shore,
 And that at length

The green and empty hills agreed
 That humankind
Might be allowed this binding deed—
 Which brings to mind

The engineering dean's reply
    To her who said,
"If such a manmade thing should lie,
    Metaled and dead

Across God's natural world, why should
    We think it best?"—
"That's a fine pendant on your God-
    created breast."

Cool repartee; but would it still
    Suffice to douse
The later, enigmatic will
    Of Mrs. Strauss?

The plaque upon his tomb displays
    The bridge; on hers
The bridgeless strait, as if she says
    That she demurs.

The yellow lupins bloom, and far below I see
    The distant cars in soundless motion.
Below the strip of road the cliffs drop brokenly
    Down to a placid blur of ocean.

High on the hill I sit and watch an errant jay
    Set a low twig of redwood swinging.
Wild columbines are here, the scent of sage and bay,
    The slanting light, a cricket singing.

IV   *Quatrains*

TELEPHONE

I see you smile across the phone
And feel the moisture of your hair
And smell the musk of your cologne . . .
Hello? Is anybody there?

GOD'S LOVE

God loves us all, I'm pleased to say—
Or those who love him anyway—
Or those who love him and are good.
Or so they say. Or so he should.

DARK ROAD

The road is dark, and home is far.
Sleep now, in the poor state you are.
Tonight be dreamless, and tomorrow
Wake free from fear, half-free of sorrow.

PIGEONS

The pigeons swing across the square,
Suddenly voiceless in midair,
Flaunting, against their civic coats,
The glossy oils that scarf their throats.

POMEGRANATE

The most impassioned of all trees,
The home of three intensities:
Gnarled trunk, dark concentrated leaf,
And flowers that burn in love and grief.

SOUTHWARD BOUND

From the gray willows of the North
Bright sprays of green now fountain forth,
For each train-hour towards Nanjing
Is two days' journey into Spring.

PENDULUM

The nervous mother shouting ceaselessly
At her roped children swinging from the tree
Remembers with a start she once was young
And terrified her mother as she swung.

ADVICE TO ORATORS

In speech it's best—though not the only way—
Indeed the best, it's true, can be the worst—
Though often I . . . as I had meant to say:
Qualify later; state the premise first.

CANT

In Cant's resilient, venerable lies
There's something for the artist to take heart.
They tell the truth that fiction never dies,
And that tradition is the soul of art.

MALEFIC THINGS

Imagining the flower pot attacked it,
The kitten flung the violets near and far.
And yet, who knows? This morning, as I backed it,
My car was set upon by a parked car.

DOOR

He dreams beyond exhaustion of a door
At which he knocked and entered years before,
But now no street or city comes to mind
Nor why he knocked, nor what he came to find.

NIGHT WATCH

Awake for hours and staring at the ceiling
Through the unsettled stillness of the night
He grows possessed of the obsessive feeling
That dawn has come and gone and brought no light.

CONDITION

I have to speak—I must—I should—I ought . . .
I'd tell you how I love you if I thought
The world would end tomorrow afternoon.
But short of that . . . well, it might be too soon.

HALF OUT OF SLEEP

Half out of sleep I watch your sleeping face.
Behind your eyelids' restlessness I see
A dream that waking may not quite displace:
If there were equity you'd dream of me.

PRANDIAL PLAINT

My love, I love your breasts. I love your nose.
I love your accent and I love your toes.
I am your slave. One word, and I obey.
But please don't slurp your coffee in that way.

INTERPRETATION

Somewhere within your loving look I sense,
Without the least intention to deceive,
Without suspicion, without evidence,
Somewhere within your heart the heart to leave.

THE END

A towel, fig bars, and a bottle of mead.
The End. I cannot grasp it, and I plead.
You cannot "keep me hanging," as you say.
Well, cut me down tomorrow, not today.

PROMISE

I will be easy company; the blur
Of what I longed for once will fade to space.
No thought that could discomfort you will stir.
My eyes will painlessly survey your face.

REUNION

If you had known . . . if I had known . . . ah well,
We played our cards so suavely, who could tell?
Ten years ago, so suavely, with such pain . . .
And, being wise, will do so once again.

PASSAGE

Your eyes, my understanding, all will rot;
The trees we see, the books we read, will go;
The way that we use words, as like as not;
And we are fortunate that this is so.

V   *Meditations of the Heart*

The gray cat stirs upon the ledge
Outside the glass doors just at dawn.
I open it; he tries to wedge
His nose indoors. It is withdrawn.
He sits back to assess my mood.
He sees me frown; he thinks of food.

I am familiar with his stunts.
His Grace, unfed, will not expire.
He may be hungry, but he hunts
When need compels him, or desire.
Just yesterday he caught a mouse
And yoyo'd it outside the house.

But now he turns his topaz eyes
Upon my eyes, which must reveal
The private pressures of these days,
The numb anxieties I feel.
But no, his grayness settles back
And yawns, and lets his limbs go slack.

He ventures forth an easy paw
As if in bargain. Thus addressed,
I fetch a bowl, and watch him gnaw
The star-shaped nuggets he likes best.
He is permitted food, and I
The furred indulgence of a sigh.

POET

for Irina Ratushinskaya

She lived for six years in a cage. When I
Am inclined to regret the way things are, I think
Of her who through long cold and pain did not
Betray the ones she loved or plead for mercy.
They censored the few letters they allowed.
Cabbage and bread, rotten and stale, were food.
While outside governments and springs went round
And summits, thaws, and great events occurred,
Here inside was no hope. Years of her youth
Were sickened for no crime. She did not even
Know if her lover knew she was alive.
The paper she'd written poems on was removed.
What could she find?—the swirls in the cold blue light
Through bars so thick her hands could not pass through
    them—
Those swirls of blue light and the heels of bread
She shared with some companionable mouse.
Her poems she memorized line by line and destroyed.
The Contents were what was difficult to remember.

ADAGIO

Fate is against me (though only in Vienna)
WOLFGANG AMADEUS MOZART, *Letters*

No need for *dolce;* once more, unemphasized,
The theme's slow clarity curves above the strings.
He does not awe us yet for while we listen
There is no more than this plain tapestry.
He never like the great Beethoven thunders,
"My stomach's aching and my heart is breaking
And you will hear me," yet to hear him is
To suffer all heartbreak, to assume all sorrow
And to survive. Where does his music cry,
"I could not sleep all night for pain. Dear friend,
Picture my situation—ill and full
Of grief and care. I am in want—could you
Assist me with a trifle? O God, here I am
With fresh entreaties instead of with thanks." . . . "Death
When we think of it is the true goal of our life."
"I could not write for very grief; black thoughts
(Which I must forcibly banish). . . ."
                                    We listen to

The adagio of the Clarinet Quintet; if
We see the abyss, as who can not, who can
Resist the enveloping tranquility
Drawn from the heart of 1789
In the clear supple lilt of one who like
The nightingale, his breast against the thorn,
Sang jubilantly in sorrow, who defied
The immobility of childhood fame

ADAGIO

To work this web of tenderness between
The freedom of a child and a man's power
Two years before an endless requiem.

The wires sink into the mist.
The red madrone trunks blur to gray.
The roadway shortens at each twist.
The headlights contradict the day.

In the bright valley that we left,
Each needle, leaf and cone distinct,
In clarity's excessive heft,
Like baffled owls we winced and blinked.

Did we expect this height might give
Far air to shape what lay below?
Or did we wish for mist to sieve
Even the nearness we should know?

Here on a lesser planet's crust
How may we hope that we exist
To mark a vision in our trust
Too bright for us and dim for mist?—

To see clear through this muffled light
That grants no needle, leaf or cone,
Or hold unchanged in changing sight
The redness of the gray madrone.

How rarely these few years, as work keeps us aloof,
    Or fares, or one thing or another,
Have we had days to spend under our parents' roof:
    Myself, my sister, and my brother.

All five of us will die; to reckon from the past
    This flesh and blood is unforgiving.
What's hard is that just one of us will be the last
    To bear it all and go on living.

THINGS

Put back the letter, half conceived
From error, half to see you grieved.
Some things are seen and disbelieved.

Some talk of failings, some of love—
That terms are reckoned from above—
What could she have been thinking of?

As if aloneness were a sign
Of greater wisdom in design
To bear the torque of me and mine.

As if the years were lists of goods,
A helve of dares, a head of shoulds
To hack a route through rotten woods.

As if creation wrapped the heart
Impenetrably in its art,
As if the land upon the chart

Were prior to the acred land
And that a mark could countermand
The houses and the trees that stand.

Though she would fell them if she could,
They will stand, and they will have stood
For all the will of dare and should.

Put it away. You cannot find
In a far reading of this kind
One character for heart or mind.

Read into things; they will remain.
Things fall apart and feel no pain.
And things, if not the world, are sane.

Voices in my head,
Chanting, "Kisses. Bread.
Prove yourself. Fight. Shove.
Learn. Earn. Look for love,"

Drown a lesser voice,
Silent now of choice:
"Breathe in peace, and be
Still, for once, like me."

I wake at three, in some slight pain.
I hear no sound of clock or rain,
No chorus of the stars, no gong,
Mosquito, siren, horn or plane.

Only my heart beats slow and strong.
I listen to its certain song.
It does not sympathize but strives
To beat all night and all day long.

Whether my spirit soars or dives,
My blood, at its compulsion, drives
Through its elastic chambers, through
My arteries, my veins, my lives.

Above all, to my heart I'm true.
It does not tell me what to do.
It beats, I live, it beats again.
For what? I wish I knew it knew.

THE WIND

The bay is thick with flecks of white.
The freezing air is honed and thinned.
The gulls sleep on the stones tonight,
Wings locked against the prizing wind.
With no companion to my mood,
Against the wind, as it should be,
I walk, but in my solitude
Bow to the wind that buffets me.

All you who sleep tonight
Far from the ones you love,
No hand to left or right,
And emptiness above—

Know that you aren't alone.
The whole world shares your tears,
Some for two nights or one,
And some for all their years.

VINTAGE INTERNATIONAL

VINTAGE INTERNATIONAL

VINTAGE INTERNATIONAL

___ **Mary** by Vladimir Nabokov	$6.95	679-72620-9
___ **Pale Fire** by Vladimir Nabokov	$9.95	679-72342-0
___ **Pnin** by Vladimir Nabokov	$7.95	679-72341-2
___ **Speak, Memory** by Vladimir Nabokov	$9.95	679-72339-0
___ **Strong Opinions** by Vladimir Nabokov	$9.95	679-72609-8
___ **Transparent Things** by Vladimir Nabokov	$6.95	679-72541-5
___ **A Bend in the River** by V. S. Naipaul	$7.95	679-72202-5
___ **Guerrillas** by V. S. Naipaul	$10.95	679-73174-1
___ **A Turn in the South** V. S. Naipaul	$9.95	679-72488-5
___ **Black Box** by Amos Oz	$8.95	679-72185-1
___ **The Shawl** by Cynthia Ozick	$7.95	679-72926-7
___ **Dictionary of the Khazars** by Milorad Pavić		
male edition	$9.95	679-72461-3
female edition	$9.95	679-72754-X
___ **Swann's Way** by Marcel Proust	$9.95	679-72009-X
___ **Kiss of the Spider Woman** by Manuel Puig	$10.00	679-72449-4
___ **Grey Is the Color of Hope**	$8.95	679-72447-8
by Irina Ratushinskaya		
___ **Memoirs of an Anti-Semite** by Gregor von Rezzori	$10.95	679-73182-2
___ **The Snows of Yesteryear** by Gregor von Rezzori	$10.95	679-73181-4
___ **The Notebooks of Malte Laurids Brigge**	$10.95	679-73245-4
by Rainer Maria Rilke		
___ **Selected Poetry** by Rainer Maria Rilke	$11.95	679-72201-7
___ **Shame** by Salman Rushdie	$9.95	679-72204-1
___ **No Exit and 3 Other Plays** by Jean-Paul Sartre	$8.95	679-72516-4
___ **All You Who Sleep Tonight** by Vikram Seth	$9.00	679-73025-7
___ **The Golden Gate** by Vikram Seth	$11.00	679-73457-0
___ **And Quiet Flows the Don** by Mikhail Sholokhov	$10.95	679-72521-0
___ **Ake: The Years of Childhood** by Wole Soyinka	$9.95	679-72540-7
___ **Ìsarà: A Voyage Around "Essay"** by Wole Soyinka	$9.95	679-73246-2
___ **Confessions of Zeno** by Italo Svevo	$9.95	679-72234-3
___ **The Beautiful Mrs. Seidenman**	$9.95	679-73214-4
by Andrzej Szczypiorski		
___ **Diary of a Mad Old Man** by Junichiro Tanizaki	$10.00	679-73024-9
___ **The Key** by Junichiro Tanizaki	$10.00	679-73023-0
___ **On the Golden Porch** by Tatyana Tolstaya	$8.95	679-72843-0
___ **The Optimist's Daughter** by Eudora Welty	$8.95	679-72883-X
___ **Losing Battles** by Eudora Welty	$8.95	679-72882-1
___ **The Eye of the Story** by Eudora Welty	$8.95	679-73004-4
___ **The Passion** by Jeanette Winterson	$8.95	679-72437-0
___ **Sexing the Cherry** by Jeanette Winterson	$9.00	679-73316-7

Available at your bookstore or call toll-free to order: 1-800-733-3000.
Credit cards only. Prices subject to change.